My Great Big Feelings

A Story for Sensitive Children

Written and illustrated by
C. M. Tolentino

Dear sensitive friends,

Being highly sensitive can feel burdensome at times. If we look closely though, we can realize all the wonderful blessings this sensitivity brings into our lives.

To my fellow parents of sensitive children – may you continue to honor and respect your children's special sensitivity. Help them learn to harness it so it may serve them well in their lives. This also goes for the grown-ups who possess this sensitivity. You and all the other sensitive humans help to make this world a more thoughtful and loving place.

For my sensitive girl.

Love, Mommy

There are times when my feelings come on quite strong.

They often cause me to feel something is wrong.

Noises can sometimes seem too loud for me.

Some places aren't as quiet as I'd like them to be.

Tags that are scratchy and clothes that itch or feel tight,

can make my body feel like something's not right.

Super bright light can also be tough.

It can be hard for my eyes to handle that stuff.

When someone around me feels angry or sad,

I can feel myself also begin to feel bad.

Some days my food feels too warm or too cold,

too soft or too chunky or too sticky to hold.

When things aren't the way I would like them to be,

uncomfortable feelings arise within me.

Having strong feelings can be so hard to do!

Have strong feelings like this ever happened to you?

It helps to know feelings are like clouds passing by.

They don't stay for long in the peaceful blue sky.

So I take a deep breath then let it out slow.

I accept all my feelings and allow them to flow.

I have learned it is special, this deep way I feel.

Having this gift is a really big deal.

It means when I'm happy I feel *that* strongly too.

I find oh so much joy in the things that I do.

Things that feel comfy as comfy can be,

are really just so extra special to me.

Since I notice and care when others feel down,

I'm a really great friend to those I'm around.

The love that I give and the love I receive,

makes my heart feel so good it's hard to believe!

It's nice to have others to help me along,

to love me and remind me my feelings aren't wrong.

It's amazing, these feelings, the good and the bad,

the upset, the loving, the happy, the sad.

Let's remember - breathe deeply and think of the sky,

as feelings come and go just like clouds passing by.

Steps for Mastering
Your Sensitivity

Step 1: Accept your feelings.
Step 2: Breathe deeply and slowly.
Step 3: Recognize your blessings.
Step 4: Let love guide you the
rest of the way.

Dear Parents,

This story was created to help sensitive children learn to cope with their sensitivity, and to help them realize the many ways in which it brings goodness into their lives.

I sincerely hope you found value in this book, and if you did I hope you will consider leaving a review for it on Amazon.com. This will increase the book's visibility and ultimately help it get into the hands of those who can truly benefit from it.

Thank you and best wishes to you and your sensitive little ones.

- C. M. Tolentino

32645165R00015